Also available in Fawcett Books:

ALSO COLLECTED BY KATHLEEN BLEASE

Love in Verse: Classic Poems of the Heart

A Friend Is Forever

PRECIOUS POEMS THAT CELEBRATE THE BEAUTY OF FRIENDSHIP

COLLECTED BY

KATHLEEN BLEASE

FAWCETT BOOKS
The Ballantine Publishing Group • New York

A Fawcett Book
Published by The Ballantine Publishing Group

Introduction and compilation copyright © 1999 by The Ballantine Publishing Group, a division of Random House, Inc.

www.randomhouse.com/BB/

Library of Congress Cataloging-in-Publication Data
A friend is forever : precious poems that celebrate the beauty of friendship / collected by Kathleen Blease. — 1st ed.
p.   cm.
Includes indexes.
ISBN 0-449-00381-7 (alk. paper)
1. Friendship—Poetry.   2. English poetry.   3. American poetry.
I. Blease, Kathleen.
PR1195.F73F75   1999
821.008'0353—dc21   98-31426
CIP

Text design by Ruth Kolbert

Cover design by Heather Kern

Manufactured in the United States of America

First Edition: February 1999

10   9   8   7   6   5   4   3   2

For there is no friend like a sister
In calm or stormy weather;
To cheer one on the tedious way,
To fetch one if one goes astray,
To lift one if one totters down,
To strengthen whilst one stands.

Christina Rossetti
(1830–1894)

CONTENTS

ACKNOWLEDGMENTS

Writers over the generations, the masters and those less celebrated alike, are truly responsible for this book. Nevertheless, the undertaking of putting together this collection required the cooperation and consideration of others. My gratitude goes to my friend, colleague, and editor Elizabeth Zack for proposing the idea, then giving me the freedom to develop it. A very special thank you goes to my husband, Roger, for his support and encouragement. This collection was constructed immediately after the birth of our second son, and Roger came to my rescue by caring for the children and the house at a moment's notice. He is truly my blessing. I can't pass this moment, of course, without showing my appreciation to the writers whose verses have endured the test of time. Once again, they are watching us enjoy their wisdom, and I'd like to thank them personally for their immortal inspiration.

INTRODUCTION

❋

YOUR TRUE FRIEND IS A VERY unique and special gift. It's difficult to imagine life without your special confidant, honest and loving, whose opinion and respect are greatly admired—and needed.

Perhaps your true friend is your sibling, spouse, or parent. Perhaps you are not related at all. Maybe you have spent your life with your true friend. Maybe you have known each other briefly. In any case, you two have connected, and without this person daily life would be burdensome, heavy, gray, silent. A true friend helps carry the load, colors the imagination, and provides a voice of comfort and celebration. And as the present quickly becomes your past, and your future stands in your doorway, it is your friend who helps you learn from what has been and eagerly greets what will be, supporting you every moment.

When you laugh and rejoice, the whole world will be with you. But when you cry, you will cry alone—that is, if it weren't for your friend, who offers you openly and willingly a place to hang and settle your grief and to mourn your losses. And when triumph comes your way, a true friend will be exhilarated by your good fortune.

Friendship has a peculiar strength. Unlike any other relationship, it can remain strong, grow and evolve even when great distances are between you. It is true that the company of a good friend is a delight and often a reprieve, but it is the friendship itself that long outlasts the good-bye. This is because friendship means to connect with another's spirit; it doesn't matter if your friend is right next door or across the country.

Whether we are aware of it or not, it is this connection between spirits that exerts a great influence on our lives. It takes our common sense—what makes us do what is right and live life calmly—and weaves into it passion and energy. In this way, friendship gives us all we need to become explorers. Feeling its invisible but unbreakable lifeline, we can brave new directions in life. And so we move out of our comfort zone into new challenges that make us grow, saving us from a life that would otherwise stagnate and be lived uneventfully and uncelebrated. Friendship makes us *thrive*!

It is easy to understand why friendship has intrigued writers for generations and has become a significant element in all literature. *A Friend Is Forever* is but a morsel of the vast offering of poetry, but between its covers is truly a celebration of the unique and powerful bond in friendship. Each poem is vivid, sometimes whimsical, and always heart-filled. Enjoy.

A Friend Is Forever

IT IS A SWEET THING

It is a sweet thing, friendship:—a dear balm;
A happy and auspicious bird of calm
Which rides o'er life's ever-tumultuous ocean;
A god that broods o'er chaos in commotion;
A flower which, fresh as Lapland roses are,
Lifts its bold head into the world's frore air,
And blooms most radiantly when others die,—
Health, hope, and youth, and brief prosperity,—
And with the light and odor of its bloom,
Shining within the dungeon and the tomb;
Whose coming is as light and music are
'Mid dissonance and gloom—a star
Which moves not mid the moving heavens alone—
A smile amid dark frowns—a gentle tone
Among rude voices, a beloved light,
A solitude, a refuge, a delight.

PERCY BYSSHE SHELLEY
[1792–1822]

WE'LL NEVER PART AGAIN

And say'st thou so? And canst thou lift
   That veil in mercy cast
Between thy destiny and thee,
   The future and the past?

Say, is it Passion's breathing vow?
   Or Friendship's promise given?
Or utterance of paternal love,
   The purest under heaven?

Oh! if thy other self be now
   Beside thee,—if thy own
That one loved hand may clasp; thy ear
   Drink in that one loved tone;

Enjoy the fleeting hour,—forget
   That earth has change or pain;—
But *dare* not whisper in thy bliss,
   "We'll never part again."

Love's roses droop ere morn hath fled;
   The violet smiles through tears;
The tall tree scatters to the blast
   The brightest leaf it bears.

Each day, each hour, love's nearest ties
    The hand of death may sever;
And they who live and love the best,
    Fate oft divides for ever.

The friend so closely link'd to thee,
    By faith so fondly plighted,—
The world's cold cautions intervene,
    And ye are disunited.

The most impassion'd love that warms
    The purest, truest heart,
Or time, or grief, or wrong may change,
    And break the links apart.

Thy children—o'er their opening minds
    Watch, watch with heart untired;
The ceaseless vigil keep, by hope,
    By love, by Heaven inspired.

Oh! beautiful the daily toil
    To work that priceless mine!
But deemest thou its golden ore
    Refined shall still be thine?

Dreamer! Those laughing boys that round
　　Thy hearth unconscious play,—
Voices already in their hearts
　　Are whispering, "Come away!"

Though warmly smile beam back to smile,
　　And answering heart to heart,
They meet in gladness who too oft
　　Have only met to part.

Then bind not earthly ties too close,
But hope let Heaven sustain;
There and there only mayst thou say,
"We'll never part again!"

ANNA MARIA WELLS
[1794–?]
———

AN EPIGRAM

You meet your friend, your face
Brightens—you have struck gold.

KASSIA
[800 A.D.]

UNDER THE GREENWOOD TREE

  *U*nder the greenwood tree,
  Who loves to lie with me,
  And turn his merry note
  Unto the sweet bird's throat,
Come hither, come hither, come hither;
    Here shall he see
    No enemy
But winter and rough weather.

  Who doth ambition shun,
  And loves to live i' the sun,
  Seeking the food he eats,
  And pleased with what he gets,
Come hither, come hither, come hither;
    Here shall he see
    No enemy
But winter and rough weather.

WILLIAM SHAKESPEARE
[1564–1616]

FRIENDSHIP

To meet a friendship such as mine,
Such feelings must the soul refine,
As are not oft of mortal birth;—
'T is love, without a stain of earth.

Looks are its food, its nectar sighs,
Its couch the lips, its throne the eyes,
The soul its breath, and so possest,
Heaven's raptures reign in mortal breast.

Though Friendship be its earthly name,
Purely from highest Heaven it came;
'T is seldom felt for more than one,
And scorns to dwell with Venus' son.

Him let it view not, or it dies
Like tender hues of morning skies,
Or morn's sweet flower, of purple glow,
When sunny beams too ardent grow.

A charm o'er every object plays—
All looks so lovely while it stays,
So softly forth, in rosier tides,
The vital flood ecstatic glides,

That, wrung by grief to see it part,
Its dearest drop escapes the heart;
Such drop, I need not tell thee, fell.
While bidding it, for thee, farewell.

MARIA A. BROOKS
[1795–1845]

A SONNET

As when with downcast eyes we muse and brood,
And ebb into a former life, or seem
To lapse far back in some confused dream
To states of mystical similitude,
If one but speaks or hems or stirs his chair,
Ever the wonder waxeth more and more,
So that we say, "All this hath been before,
All this hath been, I know not when or where";
So, friend, when first I look'd upon your face,
Our thought gave answer each to each, so true—
Opposed mirrors each reflecting each—
That, tho I knew not in what time or place,
Methought that I had often met with you,
And either lived in either's heart and speech.

ALFRED, LORD TENNYSON
[1809–1892]

A LEGACY

Friend of my many years!
When the great silence falls, at last, on me,
Let me not leave, to pain and sadden thee,
   A memory of tears,

   But pleasant thoughts alone
Of one who was thy friendship's honored guest
And drank the wine of consolation pressed
   From sorrows of thy own.

   I leave with thee a sense
Of hands upheld and trials rendered less—
The unselfish joy which is to helpfulness
   Its own great recompense;

   The knowledge that from thine,
As from the garments of the Master, stole
Calmness and strength, the virtue which makes whole
   And heals without a sign;

   Yea more, the assurance strong
That love, which fails of perfect utterance here,
Lives on to fill the heavenly atmosphere
   With its immortal song.

JOHN GREENLEAF WHITTIER
[1807–1892]

TO W. M.

❀

O tree of many branches! One thou hast
Thou barest not, but grafted'st on thee. Now,
Should all men's thunders break on thee, and leave
Thee reft of bough and blossom, that one branch
Shall cling to thee, my Father, Brother, Friend,
Shall cling to thee, until the end of end.

FRANCIS THOMPSON
[1859–1907]

GOD'S BEST GIFT

*W*hat is the best a friend can be
To any soul, to you or me?
Not only shelter, comfort, rest,
Inmost refreshment unexpressed;
Not only a beloved guide
To thread life's labyrinth at our side,
Or with love's torch lead on before;—
Though these be much, there yet is more.

The best friend is an atmosphere
Warm with all inspirations dear,
Wherein we breathe the large, free breath
Of life that has no taint of death.
Our friend is an unconscious part
Of every true beat of our heart;
A strength, a growth, whence we derive
God's health, that keeps the world alive.

The best friend is horizon, too,
Lifting unseen things into view,
And widening every petty claim
Till lost in some sublimer aim;
Blending all barriers in the great
Infinities that round us wait.
Friendship is an eternity
Where soul with soul walks, heavenly free.

Can friend lose friend? Believe it not!
The tissue whereof life is wrought,
Weaving the separate into one,
Nor end hath, nor beginning; spun
From subtle threads of destiny,
Finer than thought of man can see.
God takes not back his gifts divine;
While thy soul lives, thy friend is thine.

If but one friend has crossed thy way,
Once only, in thy mortal day;
If only once life's best surprise
Has opened on thy human eyes,—
Ingrate thou wert, indeed, if thou
Didst not in that rare presence bow,
And on earth's holy ground, unshod,
Speak softlier the dear name of *God*.

LUCY LARCOM
[1824–1893]

THE MEANS TO ATTAIN HAPPY LIFE

❁

My friend, the things that do attain
  The happy life be these, I find:
The riches left, not got with pain;
  The fruitful ground, the quiet mind;

The equal friend; no grudge, no strife;
  No charge of rule, nor governance;
Without disease the healthy life;
  The household of continuance;

The mean dièt, no dainty fare;
  Wisdom joinèd with simpleness;
The night dischargèd of all care,
  Where wine the wit may not oppress;

The faithful wife, without debate;
  Such sleeps as may beguile the night:
Content thyself with thine estate,
  Neither wish death, nor fear his might.

HENRY HOWARD, EARL OF SURREY
[1517?–1547]

WHEN TO THE SESSIONS OF SWEET SILENT THOUGHT

*W*hen to the sessions of sweet silent thought
I summon up remembrance of things past,
I sigh the lack of many a thing I sought,
And with old woes new wail my dear time's waste;
Then can I drown an eye, unused to flow,
For precious friends hid in death's dateless night,
And weep afresh love's long since cancelled woe,
And moan the expense of many a vanished sight.
Then can I grieve at grievances foregone,
And heavily from woe to woe tell o'er
The sad account of fore-bemoanëd moan,
Which I new pay as if not paid before:
  But if the while I think on thee, dear friend,
  All losses are restored, and sorrows end.

WILLIAM SHAKESPEARE
[1564–1616]

TO HIS FRIEND MASTER R. L., IN PRAISE
OF MUSIC AND POETRY

Of music and sweet poetry agree,
As they must needs, the sister and the brother,
Then must the love be great 'twixt thee and me,
Because thou lov'st the one, and I the other.
Dowland to thee is dear, whose heavenly touch
Upon the lute doth ravish human sense;
Spenser, to me, whose deep conceit is such
As, passing all conceit, needs no defence.
Thou lov'st to hear the sweet melodious sound
That Phoebus' lute, the queen of music, makes;
And I in deep delight am chiefly drowned
Whenas himself to singing he betakes:
    One god is god of both, as poets feign;
    One knight loves both, and both in thee remain.

RICHARD BARNFIELD
[1574-1627]

16

OF PERFECT FRIENDSHIP

*T*rue friendship unfeignëd
Doth rest unrestrainëd,
 No terror can tame it:
Not gaining, nor losing,
Nor gallant gay glosing,
 Can ever reclaim it.
In pain, and in pleasure,
The most truest treasure
 That may be desirëd,
Is loyal love deemëd,
Of wisdom esteemëd
 And chiefly requirëd.

HENRY CHEKE
[1548?–1586?]

BEING FORSAKEN OF HIS FRIEND HE COMPLAINETH

*W*hy should I longer long to live
   In this disease of fantasy?
Since Fortune doth not cease to give
   Things to my mind most còntrary;
And at my joys doth lour and frown
Till she hath turned them upsidown.

A friend I had, to me most dear,
   And of long time faithful and just;
There was no one my heart so near,
   Nor one in whom I had more trust;
Whom now of late, without cause why,
Fortune hath made my enemy.

The grass, methinks, should grow in sky,
   The stars unto the earth cleave fast;
The water-stream should pass awry,
   The winds should leave their strength of blast;
The sun and moon by one assent
Should both forsake the firmament;

The fish in air should fly with fin,
   The fowls in flood should bring forth fry;
All things, methinks, should erst begin
   To take their course unnaturally
Afore my friend should alter so,
Without a cause to be my foe.

———

But such is Fortune's hate, I say,
    Such is her will on me to wreak,
Such spite she hath at me alway,
    And ceaseth not my heart to break:
With such despite of cruelty,
Wherefore then longer live should I?

E. S.
[c. 1576]

OCTAVES: XV

I grant you friendship is a royal thing,
But none shall ever know that royalty
For what it is till he has realized
His best friend in himself. 'T is then, perforce,
That man's unfettered faith indemnifies
Of its own conscious freedom the old shame,
And love's revealed infinitude supplants
Of its own wealth and wisdom the old scorn.

EDWIN ARLINGTON ROBINSON
[1869–1935]

WRITTEN IN AN ALBUM
(These lines were inscribed on a leaf but two inches square.)

Thou tiny leaf,
Thou art so small, so very small,
I must be brief,
If I would sully thee at all,
With aught that from my pen may fall!

Then haste from me;
Go quick to Caroline, and show
My wish, that she
O'er no rude spot of earth, may go,
Small as thyself, where thorns shall grow;—

That there may be
No cloud so broad in all her sky
'T would shadow thee;
Nor pain nor sorrow e'er come nigh
To blanch her cheek, or dim her eye:—

That I may claim
What she on memory may bestow
In friendship's name—
A smile, or tear, as joy or wo
Shall mark the path where I may go!

HANNAH FLAGG GOULD
[1789–1865]

———

21

THE ARROW AND THE SONG

I shot an arrow into the air,
It fell to earth, I knew not where;
For, so swiftly it flew, the sight
Could not follow it in its flight.

I breathed a song into the air,
It fell to earth, I know not where;
For who has sight so knew and strong,
That it can follow the flight of song?

Long, long afterwards, in an oak
I found the arrow, still unbroke;
And the song, from beginning to end
I found again in the heart of a friend.

HENRY WADSWORTH LONGFELLOW
[1807–1882]

ON PARTING WITH A FRIEND

Can I forget thee? No, while mem'ry lasts,
Thine image like a talisman entwined,
Around my heart by sacred friendship's ties
Remains unchanged, in love, pure love, enshrined.

Can I forget thee? Childhood's happy hours
Would like some flitting phantom mock and jeer;
Life's sunny hours, would quickly lose their charm,
If Lethe's slumbrous waves but touched me there.

Can I forget thee? 'Tis a sad, sad thought,
That friend from friend should thus be ruthless
    riven—
But list, methinks, a sweet voice whispers low,
Remember, no adieus are spoke in heaven.

Can I forget thee? No, though ocean's waves
May madly leap and foam 'twixt you and me,
Still o'er my stricken heart this yearning will remain,
Nor time estrange my love, dear one, from thee.

And though on earth again we never more may meet,
In that bright Elysian where spirits, holy, dwell,
May we in concert with that transported throng,
Unite, ne'er more (rapt thought) to say "farewell!"

MARY WESTON FORDHAM
[C. 1897]

I SAW IN LOUISIANA A LIVE-OAK GROWING

I saw in Louisiana a live-oak growing,
All alone stood it and the moss hung down from the
    branches,
Without any companion it grew there uttering joyous
    leaves of dark green,
And its look, rude, unbending, lusty, made me think
    of myself,
But I wonder'd how it could utter joyous leaves stand-
    ing alone there without its friends near, for I
    knew I could not,
And I broke off a twig with a certain number of leaves
    upon it, and twined around it a little moss,
And brought it away, and I have placed it in sight in
    my room.
It is not needed to remind me of my own dear friends,
(For I believe lately I have thought of little else than of
    them)
Yet it remains to me a curious token, it makes me
    think of manly love;
For all that, and though the live-oak glistens there in
    Louisiana solitary in a wide flat space,
Uttering joyous leaves all its life without a friend or a
    lover near,
I know very well I could not.

WALT WHITMAN
[1819–1892]

IN MEMORIAM
Lines to Mrs. Isabel Peace

'Tis said but a name is friendship,
Soulless, and shallow, and vain;
That the human heart ne'er beats in response,
Or echoes sweet sympathy's strain.

But to-day in "memory's mirror"
Came a dear and honored one,
Whom in days gone by had lived and had loved,
Ere her heavenly goal was won.

Her countenance beamed as of yore,
With radiant smiles of love,
And I felt that the friendship she lavished me here,
Had ripened in heaven above.

I felt that her voice so winsome,
Attuned to holier rhymes,
Would in soft cadence tell of friendship's truth,
Like harp of a thousand strings.

Rise up and call her blest!
Ye children of her love,
For a friendlier hand or a kindlier heart
Ne'er entered the mansions above.

MARY WESTON FORDHAM
[C. 1897]

25

I GO, SWEET FRIENDS

I go, sweet friends! yet think of me
When spring's young voice awakes with flowers;
For we have wandered far and free
In those bright hours, the violet's hours.

I go; but when you pause to hear
From distant hills the Sabbath-bell
On summer-winds float silvery clear,
Think on me then—I loved it well!

Forget me not around your hearth,
When cheerly smiles the ruddy blaze;
For dear hath been its evening mirth
To me, sweet friends, in other days.

And oh! when music's voice is heard
To melt in strains of parting woe,
When hearts to love and grief are stirred,
Think of me then! I go, I go!

FELICIA HEMANS
[1793–1835]

RECONCILIATION

*Y*es, all is well. The cloud hath passed away
That hung above our friendship's path awhile;
For truth hath pierced it with a golden ray,
And love's own sunshine bathed it in a smile.

Yes, all is well, my brother. See, I place
My hand upon my late tumultuous heart,
And its soft pulses speak the cairn of peace,
Which sweetest is just after storms depart.

Now let our friendship flow, like gentle river,
With no dark stream its silver waves to stain;
And, O, let no cold wintry iceberg ever
Come floating down its summer tide again!

Let naught disturb our harmony of soul,
Let nothing come between thy heart and mine,
But let the circling years, as on they roll,
Still bring us more of sympathy divine.

We are but one remove from heavenly birth,—
Let heavenly truth be on each lip and brow;
Let us be free,—let not the dust of earth
Weigh down the white wings of our spirits now.

So when we tread Eternity's dim shore
Our souls may know each other, and rejoice
That no disguise in earthly life they wore,
And spirit voice may answer spirit voice!

GRACE GREENWOOD
[1823–1904]

MUSIC AND FRIENDSHIP

Thrice is sweet music sweet when every word
And lovely tone by kindred hearts are heard;
So when I hear true music, Heaven send,
To share that heavenly joy, one dear, dear friend!

RICHARD WATSON GILDER
[1844–1909]

OF MY FRIEND

The moonlight cloud of her invisible beauty,
    Shook from the torrent glory of her soul
In aëry spray, hangs round her; love grows duty,
    If you that angel-populous aureole
            Have the glad power to feel;
            As all our longings kneel
To the intense and cherub-wingèd stole
Orbing a painted Saint: and through control
            Of this sweet faint
            Veil, my unguessing Saint
Celestial ministrations sheds which heal.

Now, Friend, short sweet outsweetening sharpest
            woes!
    In wintry cold a little, little flame—
So much to me that little!—here I close
    This errant song. O pardon its much blame!
            Now my grey day grows bright
            A little ere the night;
Let after-livers who may love my name,
And gauge the price I paid for dear-bought fame,
            Know that at end,
            Pain was well paid, sweet Friend,
Pain was well paid which brought me to your sight.

FRANCIS THOMPSON
[1859–1907]

FRIENDSHIP

A ruddy drop of manly blood
The surging sea outweighs,
The world uncertain comes and goes;
The lover rooted stays.
I fancied he was fled,—
And, after many a year,
Glowed unexhausted kindliness,
Like daily sunrise there.
My careful heart was free again,
O friend, my bosom said,
Through thee alone the sky is arched,
Through thee the rose is red;
All things through thee take nobler form,
And look beyond the earth,
The mill-round of our fate appears
A sun-path in thy worth.
Me too thy nobleness has taught
To master my despair;
The fountains of my hidden life
Are through thy friendship fair.

RALPH WALDO EMERSON
[1803–1882]

TRUE FRIENDS

True friends,
Like ivy and the wall,
Both stand together,
And together fall.

THOMAS CARLYLE
[1795–1881]

A SONG
(Written in her fifteenth year.)

❁

Life is but a troubled ocean,
Hope a meteor, love a flower
Which blossoms in the morning beam,
And withers with the evening hour.

Ambition is a dizzy height,
And glory, but a lightning gleam;
Fame is a bubble, dazzling bright,
Which fairest shines in fortune's beam.

When clouds and darkness veil the skies,
And sorrow's blast blows loud and chill,
Friendship shall like a rainbow rise,
And softly whisper—peace, be still.

LUCRETIA MARIA DAVIDSON
[1808–1825]

AT THE GRAVE OF BURNS *(Excerpts)*

I mourned with thousands, but as one
More deeply grieved, for He was gone
Whose light I hailed when first it shone,
  And showed my youth
How Verse may build a princely throne
  On humble truth.

True friends though diversely inclined;
But heart with heart and mind with mind,
Where the main fibers are entwined,
  Through Nature's skill,
May even by contraries be joined
  More closely still.

The tear will start, and let it flow;
Thou "poor Inhabitant below,"
At this dread moment—even so—
  Might we together
Have sate and talked where gowans blow,[1]
  Or on wild heather.

[1]*Gowans blow.* Daisies bloom.

WILLIAM WORDSWORTH
[1770–1850]

34

SONNETS FROM THE PORTUGUESE
Sonnet 2

*B*ut only three in all God's universe
Have heard this word thou hast said,—Himself, beside
Thee speaking, and me listening! and replied
One of us . . . that was God, . . . and laid the curse
So darkly on my eyelids, as to amerce
My sight from seeing thee,—that if I had died,
The deathweights, placed there, would have signified
Less absolute exclusion. "Nay" is worse
From God than from all others, O my friend!
Men could not part us with their worldly jars,
Nor the seas change us, nor the tempests bend;
Our hands would touch for all the mountain-bars:
And, heaven being rolled between us at the end,
We should but vow the faster for the stars.

ELIZABETH BARRETT BROWNING
[1770–1850]

TO MRS. M. A. AT PARTING

1.

ℐ have examin'd and do find,
   Of all that favour me
There's none I grieve to leave behind
   But only only thee.
To part with thee I needs must die,
   Could parting sep'rate thee and I.

2.

But neither Chance nor Complement
   Did element our Love;
'Twas sacred Sympathy was lent
   Us from the Quire above.
That Friendship Fortune did create,
   Still fears a wound from Time or Fate.

3.

Our chang'd and mingled Souls are grown
   To such acquaintance now,
That if each would resume their own,
   Alas! we know not how.
We have each other so engrost,
   That each is in the Union lost.

———

4.

And thus we can no Absence know,
  Nor shall we be confin'd;
Our active Souls will daily go
  To learn each others mind.
Nay, should we never meet to Sense,
  Our Souls would hold Intelligence.

5.

Inspired with a Flame Divine
  I scorn to court a stay;
For from that noble Soul of thine
  I ne're can be away.
But I shall weep when thou dost grieve;
  Nor can I die whil'st thou dost live.

6.

By my own temper I shall guess
  At thy felicity,
And only like my happiness
  Because it pleaseth thee.
Our hearts at any time will tell
  If thou, or I, be sick, or well.

———

7.

All Honour sure I must pretend,
   All that is Good or Great;
She that would be *Rosania*'s Friend,
   Must be at least compleat.
If I have any bravery,
   'Tis cause I have so much of thee.

8.

Thy Leiger Soul in me shall lie,
   And all thy thoughts reveal;
Then back again with mine shall flie,
   And thence to me shall steal.
Thus still to one another tend;
   Such is the sacred name of *Friend*.

9.

Thus our twin-Souls in one shall grow,
   And teach the World new Love,
Redeem the Age and Sex, and shew
   A Flame Fate dares not move:
And courting Death to be our friend,
   Our Lives together too shall end.

———

10.

A Dew shall dwell upon our Tomb
   Of such a quality,
That fighting Armies, thither come,
   Shall reconciled be.
We'll ask no Epitaph, but say
   ORINDA and ROSANIA.

KATHERINE PHILIPS
[1631–1664]

WHO?

My friend must be a bird,
Because it flies!
Mortal my friend must be,
Because it dies!
Barbs has it, like a bee.
Ah, curious friend,
Thou puzzlest me!

EMILY DICKINSON
[1830–1886]

THE PRESENT AGE

Say not the age is hard and cold—
   I think it brave and grand;

When men of diverse sects and creeds
   Are clasping hand in hand.

The Parsee from his sacred fires
   Beside the Christian kneels;

And clearer light to Islam's eyes
   The word of Christ reveals.

The Brahmin from his distant home
   Brings thoughts of ancient lore;

The Bhuddist breaking bonds of caste
   Divides mankind no more.

The meek-eyed sons of far Cathay
   Are welcome round the board;

Not greed, nor malice drives away
   These children of our Lord.

And Judah from whose trusted hands
    Came oracles divine;

Now sits with those around whose hearts
    The light of God doth shine.

Japan unbars her long sealed gates
    From islands far away;

Her sons are lifting up their eyes
    To greet the coming day.

The Indian child from forests wild
    Has learned to read and pray;

The tomahawk and scalping knife
    From him have passed away.

From centuries of servile toil
    The Negro finds release,

And builds the fanes of prayer and praise
    Unto the God of Peace.

England and Russia face to face
　　With Central Asia meet;

And on the far Pacific coast,
　　Chinese and natives greet.

Crusaders once with sword and shield
　　The Holy Land to save;

From Moslem hands did strive to clutch
　　The dear Redeemer's grave.

A battle greater, grander far
　　Is for the present age;

A crusade for the rights of man
　　To brighten history's page.

Where labor faints and bows her head,
　　And want consorts with crime;

Or men grown faithless sadly say
　　That evil is the time.

———

There is the field, the vantage ground
   For every earnest heart;

To side with justice, truth and right
   And act a noble part.

To save from ignorance and vice
   The poorest, humblest child;

To make our age the fairest one
   On which the sun has smiled.

To plant the roots of coming years
   In mercy, love and truth;

And bid our weary, saddened earth
   Again renew her youth.

Oh! earnest hearts! toil on in hope,
   'Till darkness shrinks from light;

To fill the earth with peace and joy,
   Let youth and age unite:

To stay the floods of sin and shame
   That sweep from shore to shore;

And furl the banners stained with blood,
   'Till war shall be no more.

Blame not the age, nor think it full
   Of evil and unrest;

But say of every other age,
   "This one shall be the best."

The age to brighten every path
   By sin and sorrow trod;

For loving hearts to usher in
   The commonwealth of God.

FRANCES E. W. HARPER
[1825–1911]

NOT HEAT FLAMES UP AND CONSUMES

❀

*N*ot heat flames up and consumes,
Not sea-waves hurry in and out,
Not the air, delicious and dry, the air of the ripe
      summer, bears lightly along white down-balls
      of myriads of seeds,
Wafted, sailing gracefully, to drop where they may;
Not these—O none of these, more than the flames of
      me, consuming, burning for his love whom I
      love!
O none, more than I, hurrying in and out:
—Does the tide hurry, seeking something, and never
      give up? O I the same;
O nor down-balls, nor perfumes, nor the high,
      rain-emitting clouds, are borne through the
      open air,
Any more than my Soul is borne through the open air,
Wafted in all directions, O love, for friendship, for you.

WALT WHITMAN
[1819–1892]

———

FRIENDSHIP AFTER LOVE

After the fierce midsummer all ablaze
  Has burned itself to ashes, and expires
  In the intensity of its own fires,
There come the mellow, mild, St. Martin days
Crowned with the calm of peace, but sad with haze.
  So after Love has led us, till he tires
  Of his own throes, and torments, and desires,
Comes large-eyed friendship: with a restful gaze,
He beckons us to follow, and across
  Cool verdant vales we wander free from care.
  Is it a touch of frost lies in the air?
Why are we haunted with a sense of loss?
We do not wish the pain back, or the heat;
And yet, and yet, these days are incomplete.

ELLA WHEELER WILCOX
[1850–1919]

TO MRS. P——,

With Some Drawings of Birds and Insects (Excerpts)

The kindred arts to please thee shall conspire,
One dip the pencil, and one string the lyre.

—POPE

1

*A*manda bids;—at her command again
I seize the pencil, or resume the pen;
No other call my willing hand requires,
And Friendship, better than a Muse inspires.

2

Painting and Poetry are near allied;
The kindred arts two sister Muses guide:
This charms the eye, that steals upon the ear;
There sounds are tuned, and colours blended here:
This with a silent touch enchants our eyes,
And bids a gayer, brighter world arise:
That, less allied to sense, with deeper art
Can pierce the close recesses of the heart;
By well-set syllables, and potent sound,
Can rouse, can chill the breast, can soothe, can wound;
To life adds motion, and to beauty soul,
And breathes a spirit through the finished whole:
Each perfects each, in friendly union joined;—
This gives Amanda's form, and that her mind.

3

But humbler themes my artless hand requires,
No higher than the feathered tribe aspires.
Yet who the various nations can declare
That plough with busy wing the peopled air?
These cleave the crumbling bark for insect food;
Those dip their crooked beak in kindred blood:
Some haunt the rushy moor, the lonely woods;
Some bathe their silver plumage in the floods;
Some fly to man, his household gods implore,
And gather round his hospitable door,
Wait the known call, and find protection there
From all the lesser tyrants of the air.

9

Thy friend thus strives to cheat the lonely hour,
With song or paint, an insect or a flower:—
Yet if Amanda praise the flowing line,
And bend delighted o'er the gay design,
I envy not nor emulate the fame
Or of the painter's or the poet's name:
Could I to both with equal claim pretend,
Yet far, far dearer were the name of Friend.

ANNA LÆTITIA BARBAULD
[1743–1825]

A SHROPSHIRE LAD *(Excerpt)*

CLEE HILL

You and I must keep from shame
In London streets the Shropshire name;
On banks of Thames they must not say
Severn breeds worse men than they;
And friends abroad must bear in mind
Friends at home they leave behind.
Oh, I shall be stiff and cold
When I forget you, hearts of gold;
The land where I shall mind you not
Is the land where all's forgot.
And if my foot returns no more
To Teme nor Corve nor Severn shore,
Luck, my lads, be with you still
By falling stream and standing hill,
By chiming tower and whispering tree,
Men that made a man of me.
About your work in town and farm
Still you'll keep my head from harm,
Still you'll help me, hands that gave
A grasp to friend me to the grave.

ALFRED EDWARD HOUSMAN
[1859–1936]

MEDICINE SONGS
Transcribed from the Indian Originals

THE HEART'S FRIEND

Fair is the white star of twilight,
and the sky clearer
At the day's end;
But she is fairer, and she is dearer.
She, my heart's friend!

Far stars and fair in the skies bending,
Low stars of hearth fires and wood smoke ascending,
The meadow-lark's nested,
The night hawk is winging;
Home through the star-shine the hunter comes
        singing.

Fair is the white star of twilight,
And the moon roving
To the sky's end;
But she is fairer, better worth loving,
She, my heart's friend.
—*Shoshone Love Song*

A SONG IN TIME OF DEPRESSION

Now all my singing Dreams are gone,
But none knows where they have fled
Nor by what trails they have left me.

Return, O Dreams of my heart,
And sing in the Summer twilight,
By the creek and the almond thicket
And the field that is bordered with lupins!

Now is my refuge to seek
In the hollow of friendly shoulders,
Since the singing is stopped in my pulse
And the earth and the sky refuse me;
Now must I hold by the eyes of a friend
When the high white stars are unfriendly.

Over-sweet is the refuge for trusting;
Return and sing, O my Dreams,
In the dewy and palpitant pastures,
Till the love of living awakes
And the strength of the hills to uphold me.
—*From the Paiute*

MARY AUSTIN
[1868–1934]

———

LINES ADDRESSED TO A COUSIN

She gave me a flow'ret,—and oh! it was sweet!
'T was a pea, in full bloom, with its dark crimson leaf,
And I said in my heart, this shall be thy retreat!
'T is one "sacred to Friendship"—a stranger to grief.

In my bosom I placed it,—'t is withered and gone!
All its freshness, its beauty, its fragrance had fled!
And in sorrow I sigh'd,—am I *thus* left alone?
Is the gift which I cherish'd quite faded and dead?

It has wither'd! but *she* who presented it blooms,
Still fresh and unfading, in memory *here*
And through life shall *here* flourish, 'mid danger and
        storms,
As sweet as the flower, though more lasting and fair!

LUCRETIA MARIA DAVIDSON
[1808–1825]

AULD LANG SYNE *(Excerpts)*

Should auld acquaintance be forgot,
   And never brought to min'?
Should auld acquaintance be forgot,
   And auld lang syne?

For auld lang syne, my dear.
   For auld lang syne,
We'll tak a cup o' kindness yet,
   For auld lang syne.

And there's a hand, my trusty fiere,
   And gie 's a hand o' thine:
And we'll tak a right guid-willie waught,[1]
   For auld lang syne.

And surely ye'll be your pint-stowp,
   And surely I'll be mine;
And we'll tak a cup o' kindness yet
   For auld lang syne.

[1]good draught

ROBERT BURNS
[1759–1796]

THE THREE SORTS OF FRIENDS
(Excerpt)

*T*hough friendships differ endless *in degree*,
The *sorts*, methinks, may be reduced to three.
Ac quaintance many, and *Con* quaintance few;
But for *In* quaintance I know only two—
The friend I've mourned with, and the maid I woo!

SAMUEL TAYLOR COLERIDGE
[1772–1834]

TO NOTHING FITTER

To nothing fitter can I thee compare
Than to the son of some rich pennyfather,
Who having now brought on his end with care,
Leaves to his son all he had heaped together;
This new-rich novice, lavish of his chest,
To one man gives, doth on another spend,
Then here he riots, yet amongst the rest
Haps to lend some to one true honest friend.
Thy gifts thou in obscurity dost waste,
False friends thy kindness, born but to deceive thee,
Thy love, that is on the unworthy placed,
Time hath thy beauty, which with age will leave thee;
Only that little which to me was lent
I give thee back, when all the rest is spent.

MICHAEL DRAYTON
[1563–1631]

THE GOOD, GREAT MAN

✾

"How seldom, friend! a good great man inherits
　　Honour or wealth with all his worth and pains!
It sounds like stories from the land of spirits
If any man obtain that which he merits
　　Or any merit that which he obtains."

REPLY TO THE ABOVE

For shame, dear friend, renounce this canting
　　　strain!
What would'st thou have a good great man obtain?
Place? titles? salary? a gilded chain?
Or throne of corses which his sword had slain?
Greatness and goodness are not *means*, but *ends*!
Hath he not always treasures, always friends,
The good great man? *three* treasures, LOVE,
　　　and LIGHT,
　　And CALM THOUGHTS, regular as infant's
　　　breath:
And three firm friends, more sure than day and night,
　　HIMSELF, his MAKER, and the ANGEL DEATH!

SAMUEL TAYLOR COLERIDGE
[1772–1834]

———

FRIENDSHIP'S MYSTERY, TO MY DEAREST LUCASIA

1.

Come, my *Lucasia*, since we see
   That Miracles Mens faith do move,
   By wonder and by prodigy
To the dull angry world let's prove
   There's a Religion in our Love.

2.

For though we were design'd t' agree,
   That Fate no liberty destroyes,
But our Election is as free
   As Angels, who with greedy choice
   Are yet determin'd to their joyes.

3.

Our hearts are doubled by the loss,
   Here Mixture is Addition grown;
We both diffuse, and both ingross:
   And we whose minds are so much one,
   Never, yet ever are alone.

4.

We court our own Captivity
   Than Thrones more great and innocent:
'Twere banishment to be set free,
   Since we wear fetters whose intent
   Not Bondage is, but Ornament.

5.

Divided joyes are tedious found,
   And griefs united easier grow:
We are our selves but by rebound,
   And all our Titles shuffled so,
   Both Princes, and both Subjects too.

6.

Our Hearts are mutual Victims laid,
   While they (such power in Friendship lies)
Are Altars, Priests, and Off 'rings made:
   And each Heart which thus kindly dies,
   Grows deathless by the Sacrifice.

KATHERINE PHILIPS
[1631–1664]

TO MY EXCELLENT LUCASIA, ON OUR FRIENDSHIP

I did not live until this time
  Crown'd my felicity,
When I could say without a crime,
  I am not thine, but thee.

This carcass breath'd, and walkt, and slept,
  So that the world believ'd
There was a soul the motions kept;
  But they were all deceiv'd.

For as a watch by art is wound
  To motion, such was mine:
But never had Orinda found
  A soul till she found thine;

Which now inspires, cures and supplies,
  And guides my darkned breast:
For thou art all that I can prize,
  My joy, my life, my rest.

No bridegroom's nor crown-conqueror's mirth
  To mine compar'd can be:
They have but pieces of the earth,
  I've all the world in thee.

Then let our flames still light and shine,
    And no false fear controul,
As innocent as our design,
    Immortal as our soul.

KATHERINE PHILIPS
[1631–1664]

PARTING WITH LUCASIA: A SONG

I

*W*ell, we will do that rigid thing
   Which makes spectators think we part;
Though Absence hath for none a sting
   But those who keep each other's heart.

II

And when our sense is dispossest,
   Our labouring souls will heave and pant,
And gasp for one another's breast,
   Since their conveyances they want.

III

Nay, we have felt the tedious smart
   Of absent Friendship, and do know
That when we die we can but part;
   And who knows what we shall do now?

IV

Yet I must go: we will submit,
   And so our own disposers be;
For while we nobly suffer it,
   We triumph o'er Necessity.

V

By this we shall be truly great,
  If having other things o'ercome,
To make our victory complete
  We can be conquerors at home.

VI

Nay then to meet we may conclude,
  And all obstructions overthrow,
Since we our passion have subdu'd,
  Which is the strongest thing I know.

KATHERINE PHILIPS
[1631–1664]

ALAS, 'TIS TRUE I HAVE GONE
HERE AND THERE

Alas, 'tis true, I have gone here and there
And made myself a motley to the view,
Gor'd mine own thoughts, sold cheap what is most
     dear,
Made old offences of affections new.
Most true it is that I have look'd on truth
Askance and strangely: but, by all above,
These blenches gave my heart another youth,
And worse essays prov'd thee my best of love.
Now all is done, have what shall have no end!
Mine appetite, I never more will grind
On newer proof, to try an older friend,
A god in love, to whom I am confin'd.
  Then give me welcome, next my heaven the best,
  Even to thy pure and most most loving breast.

THE FOUNTAIN

❁

A CONVERSATION

*W*e talked with open heart and tongue
Affectionate and true,
A pair of friends, though I was young,
And Matthew seventy-two.

We lay beneath a spreading oak,
Beside a mossy seat;
And from the turf a fountain broke,
And gurgled at our feet.

"Now, Matthew!" said I, "let us match
This water's pleasant tune
With some old border-song, or catch,
That suits a summer's noon;

"Or of the church-clock and the chimes
Sing here beneath the shade,
That half-mad thing of witty rhymes
Which you last April made!"

In silence Matthew lay, and eyed
The spring beneath the tree;
And thus the dear old Man replied,
The grey-haired man of glee:

"No check, no stay, this Streamlet fears;
How merrily it goes!
'Twill murmur on a thousand years,
And flow as now it flows.

"And here, on this delightful day,
I cannot choose but think
How oft, a vigorous man, I lay
Beside this fountain's brink.

"My eyes are dim with childish tears,
My heart is idly stirred,
For the same sound is in my ears
Which in those days I heard.

"Thus fares it still in our decay:
And yet the wiser mind
Mourns less for what age takes away
Than what it leaves behind.

"The blackbird amid leafy trees,
The lark above the hill,
Let loose their carols when they please,
Are quiet when they will.

"With Nature never do *they* wage
A foolish strife; they see
A happy youth, and their old age
Is beautiful and free:

"But we are pressed by heavy laws;
And often, glad no more,
We wear a face of joy, because
We have been glad of yore.

"If there be one who need bemoan
His kindred laid in earth,
The household hearts that were his own;
It is the man of mirth.

"My days, my Friend, are almost gone,
My life has been approved,
And many love me; but by none
Am I enough beloved."

"Now both himself and me he wrongs,
The man who thus complains;
I live and sing my idle songs
Upon these happy plains;

"And, Matthew, for thy children dead
I'll be a son to thee!"
At this he grasped my hand, and said,
"Alas! that cannot be."

We rose up from the fountain-side;
And down the smooth descent
Of the green sheep-track did we glide;
And through the wood we went;

And, ere we came to Leonard's-rock,
We sang those witty rhymes
About the crazy old church-clock,
And the bewildered chimes.

WILLIAM WORDSWORTH
[1770–1850]

LITTLE THINGS

❀

_L_ittle drops of water,
Little grains of sand,
Make the mighty ocean
And the pleasant land.

Little deeds of kindness,
Little words of love,
Make our world an Eden
Like the Heaven above.

JULIA CARNEY
[1823–1908]

POLONIUS' ADVICE TO HIS SON

These few precepts in thy memory
See thou character. Give thy thoughts no tongue,
Nor any unproportion'd thought his act.
Be thou familiar, but by no means vulgar:
The friends thou hast, and their adoption tried,
Grapple them to thy soul with hoops of steel;
But do not dull thy palm with entertainment
Of each new-hatch'd, unfledg'd comrade. Beware
Of entrance to a quarrel: but being in,
Bear't that th' opposed may beware of thee.
Give every man thine ear, but few thy voice:
Take each man's censure, but reserve thy judgment.
Costly thy habit as thy purse can buy,
But not express'd in fancy: rich, not gaudy;
For the apparel oft proclaims the man.
Neither a borrower nor a lender be;
For loan oft loses both itself and friend,
And borrowing dulls the edge of husbandry.
This above all: to thine own self be true;
And it must follow, as the night the day,
Thou canst not then be false to any man.

WILLIAM SHAKESPEARE
[1564–1616]

IF I SHOULD DIE TONIGHT

If I should die tonight,
My friends would look upon my quiet face
Before they laid it in its resting place,
And deem that death had left it almost fair;
And laying snow-white flowers against my hair,
Would smooth it down with tearful tenderness,
And fold my hands with lingering caress;
Poor hands, so empty and so cold tonight!

If I should die tonight,
My friends would call to mind with loving thought,
Some kindly deed the icy hand had wrought,
Some gentle word the frozen lips had said;
Errands on which the willing feet had sped.
The memory of my selfishness and pride,
My hasty words, would all be put aside,
And so I should be loved and mourned tonight.

If I should die tonight,
Even hearts estranged would turn once more to me.
Recalling other days remorsefully.
The eyes that chill me with averted glance
Would look upon me as of yore, perchance,
Would soften in the old, familiar way;
For who could war with dumb, unconscious clay?
So I might rest, forgiven of all, tonight.

O friends, I pray tonight,
Keep not your kisses for my dead, cold brow.
The way is lonely; let me feel them now.
Think gently of me; I am travel-worn;
My faltering feet are pierced with many a thorn.
Forgive, O hearts estranged, forgive, I plead!
When dreamless rest is mine I shall not need
The tenderness for which I long tonight.

ARABELLA EUGENIA SMITH
[1845–1916]

WHAT IS GOOD?

"What is the real good?"
I ask in musing mood.

"Order," said the law court;
"Knowledge," said the school;
"Truth," said the wise man;
"Pleasure," said the fool;
"Love," said the maiden;
"Beauty," said the page;
"Freedom," said the dreamer;
"Home," said the sage;
"Fame," said the soldier;
"Equity," said the seer.
Spake my heart fully sad:
"The answer is not here."

Then within my bosom
Softly this I heard:
"Each heart holds the secret:
'Kindness' is the word."

JOHN BOYLE O'REILLY
[1844–1890]

MY OLD FRIEND

*Y*ou've a manner all so mellow,
My old friend,
That it cheers and warms a fellow,
My old friend,
Just to meet and greet you, and
Feel the pressure of a hand
That one may understand,
My old friend.

Though dimmed in youthful splendor,
My old friend,
Your smiles are still as tender,
My old friend,
And your eyes as true a blue
As your childhood ever knew,
And your laugh as merry, too,
My old friend.

For though your hair is faded,
My old friend,
And your step a trifle jaded,
My old friend,
Old time, with all his lures
In the trophies he secures,
Leaves young that heart of yours,
My old friend.

And so it is you cheer me,
My old friend,
For to know you and be near you,
My old friend,
Makes my hopes of clearer light,
And my faith of surer sight,
And my soul a purer white,
My old friend.

JAMES WHITCOMB RILEY
[1849–1916]

FRIENDSHIP'S LIKE MUSIC *(Excerpts)*

Friendship's like music; two strings tuned alike,
Will both stir, though but only one you strike.
It is the quintessence of all perfection
Extracted into one: a sweet connection
Of all the virtues moral and divine,
Abstracted into one. It is a mine,
Whose nature is not rich, unless in making
The state of others wealthy, by partaking.
It blooms and blossoms both in sun and shade,
Doth (like a bay in winter) never fade:
It loveth all, and yet suspecteth none,
Is provident, yet seeketh not her own;
'Tis rare itself, yet maketh all things common;
And is judicious, yet judgeth no man.

The perfect model of true friendship's this:
A rare affection of the soul, which is
Begun with ripened judgment; doth persever
With simple wisdom, and concludes with Never.
'Tis pure in substance, as refined gold,
That buyeth all things, but is never sold,
It is a coin, and most men walk without it;
True love's the stamp, Jehovah's writ about it;
It rusts unused, but using makes it brighter,
'Gainst Heaven high treason 'tis to make it lighter.

FRANCIS QUARLES
[1592–1644]

MY HEART WAS COMFORTED

One came and told me suddenly,
"Your friend is dead! Last year she went";
But many years my friend had spent
In life's wide wastes, apart from me.

And lately I had felt her near,
And walked as if by soft winds fanned,
Had felt the touching of her hand,
Had known she held me close and dear.

And swift I learned that being dead
Meant rather being free to live,
And free to seek me, free to give,
And so my heart was comforted.

MARGARET E. SANGSTER
[1838–1912]

FRIENDS OF YOUTH

The half-seen memories of childish days,
When pains and pleasures lightly came and went;
The sympathies of boyhood rashly spent
In fearful wanderings through forbidden ways;
The vague, but manly wish to tread the maze
Of life to noble ends,—whereon intent,
Asking to know for what man here is sent,
The bravest heart must often pause and gaze;
The firm resolve to seek the chosen end
Of manhood's judgment, cautious and mature,—
Each of these viewless bonds binds friend to friend
With strength no selfish purpose can secure:
My happy lot is this, that all attend
That friendship which first came and which shall last
      endure.

AUBREY THOMAS DE VERE
[1814–1902]

SILENCE

'Tis better to sit here beside the sea,
Here on the spray-kissed beach,
In silence, that between such friends as we
Is full of deepest speech.

PAUL LAURENCE DUNBAR
[1872–1906]

Dear friend, I pray thee, if thou wouldst be proving
Thy strong regard for me,
Make me no vows. Lip-service is not loving;
Let thy faith speak for thee.

Swear not to me that nothing can divide us—
So little such oaths mean.
But when distrust and envy creep beside us,
Let them not come between.

Say not to me the depths of thy devotion
Are deeper than the sea;
But watch, lest doubt or some unkind emotion
Embitter them for thee.

Vow not to love me ever and forever,
Words are such idle things;
But when we differ in opinions, never
Hurt me by little stings.

I'm sick of words: they are so lightly spoken,
And spoken, are but air.
I'd rather feel thy trust in me unbroken
Than list thy words so fair.

If all the little proofs of trust are heeded,
If thou art always kind.
No sacrifice, no promise will be needed
To satisfy my mind.

ELLA WHEELER WILCOX
[1855–1919]

LIFE'S MIRROR

There are loyal hearts, there are spirits brave,
There are souls that are pure and true;
Then give to the world the best you have,
And the best will come back to you.

Give love, and love to your life will flow,
A strength in your utmost need;
Have faith, and a score of hearts will show
Their faith in your work and deed.

Give truth, and your gift will be paid in kind,
And honor will honor meet;
And the smile which is sweet will surely find
A smile that is just as sweet.

Give sorrow and pity to those who mourn;
You will gather in flowers again
The scattered seeds from your thought outborne,
Though the sowing seemed but vain.

For life is the mirror of king and slave,
'Tis just what we are and do;
Then give to the world the best you have
And the best will come back to you.

MADELINE S. BRIDGES
[1844–1920]

HOME, SWEET HOME

Sharers of a common country,
　　They had met in deadly strife;

Men who should have been as brothers
　　Madly sought each other's life.

In the silence of the even,
　　When the cannon's lips were dumb,

Thoughts of home and all its loved ones
　　To the soldier's heart would come.

On the margin of a river,
　　'Mid the evening's dews and damps,

Could be heard the sounds of music
　　Rising from two hostile camps.

One was singing of its section
　　Down in Dixie, Dixie's land,

And the other of the banner
　　Waved so long from strand to strand.

In the land where Dixie's ensign
    Floated o'er the hopeful slave,

Rose the song that freedom's banner,
    Starry-lighted, long might wave.

From the fields of strife and carnage,
    Gentle thoughts began to roam,

And a tender strain of music
    Rose with words of "Home, Sweet Home."

Then the hearts of strong men melted,
    For amid our grief and sin

Still remains that "touch of nature,"
    Telling us we all are kin.

In one grand but gentle chorus,
    Floating to the starry dome,

Came the words that brought them nearer,
    Words that told of "Home, Sweet Home."

For awhile, all strife forgotten,
    They were only brothers then,

Joining in the sweet old chorus,
    Not as soldiers, but as men.

Men whose hearts would flow together,
    Though apart their feet might roam,

Found a tie they could not sever,
    In the mem'ry of each home.

Never may the steps of carnage
    Shake our land from shore to shore,

But may mother, home and Heaven,
    Be our watchwords evermore.

FRANCES E. W. HARPER
[1825–1911]

TRUE FRIENDSHIP

A kind mouth multiplies friends,
   and gracious lips prompt friendly greetings.
Let your acquaintances be many,
   but one in a thousand your confidant. . . .
A faithful friend is a sturdy shelter;
   he who finds one finds a treasure.
A faithful friend is beyond price,
   no sum can balance his worth.
A faithful friend is a life-saving remedy,
   such as he who fears God finds;
For he who fears God behaves accordingly,
   and his friend will be like himself.

THE BIBLE

MY PLAYMATE

The pines were dark on Ramoth hill,
  Their song was soft and low;
The blossoms in the sweet May wind
  Were falling like the snow.

The blossoms drifted at our feet,
  The orchard birds sang clear;
The sweetest and the saddest day
  It seemed of all the year.

For, more to me than birds or flowers,
  My playmate left her home,
And took with her the laughing spring,
  The music and the bloom.

She kissed the lips of kith and kin,
  She laid her hand in mine:
What more could ask the bashful boy
  Who fed her father's kine?

She left us in the bloom of May:
  The constant years told o'er
Their seasons with as sweet May morns,
  But she came back no more.

I walk, with noiseless feet, the round
　　Of uneventful years;
Still o'er and o'er I sow the spring
　　And reap the autumn ears.

She lives where all the golden year
　　Her summer roses blow;
The dusky children of the sun
　　Before her come and go.

There haply with her jewelled hands
　　She smooths her silken gown,—
No more the homespun lap wherein
　　I shook the walnuts down.

The wild grapes wait us by the brook,
　　The brown nuts on the hill,
And still the May-day flowers make sweet
　　The woods of Follymill.

The lilies blossom in the pond,
　　The bird builds in the tree,
The dark pines sing on Ramoth hill
　　The slow song of the sea.

I wonder if she thinks of them,
    And how the old time seems,—
If ever the pines of Ramoth wood
    Are sounding in her dreams.

I see her face, I hear her voice;
    Does she remember mine?
And what to her is now the boy
    Who fed her father's kine?

What cares she that the orioles build
    For other eyes than ours,—
That other hands with nuts are filled,
    And other laps with flowers?

O playmate in the golden time!
    Our mossy seat is green,
Its fringing violets blossom yet,
    The old trees o'er it lean.

The winds so sweet with birch and fern
    A sweeter memory blow;
And there in spring the veeries sing
    The song of long ago.

———

And still the pines of Ramoth wood
   Are moaning like the sea,—
The moaning of the sea of change
   Between myself and thee!

JOHN GREENLEAF WHITTIER
[1807–1892]

BILL AND JOE

Come, dear old comrade, you and I
Will steal an hour from days gone by,
The shining days when life was new,
And all was bright with morning dew,
The lusty days of long ago,
When you were Bill and I was Joe.

Your name may flaunt a titled trail
Proud as a cockerel's rainbow tail,
And mine as brief appendix wear
As Tam O'Shanter's luckless mare;
To-day, old friend, remember still
That I am Joe and you are Bill.

You've won the great world's envied prize,
And grand you look in people's eyes,
With HON. and LL.D.
In big brave letters, fair to see,—
Your fist, old fellow! off they go!—
How are you, Bill? How are you, Joe?

You've worn the judge's ermined robe;
You've taught your name to half the globe;
You've sung mankind a deathless strain;
You've made the dead past live again:
The world may call you what it will,
But you and I are Joe and Bill.

The chaffing young folks stare and say
"See those old buffers, bent and gray,—
They talk like fellows in their teens!
Mad, poor old boys! That's what it means,"—
And shake their heads; they little know
The throbbing hearts of Bill and Joe!—

How Bill forgets his hour of pride,
While Joe sits smiling at his side;
How Joe, in spite of time's disguise,
Finds the old schoolmate in his eyes,—
Those calm, stern eyes that melt and fill
As Joe looks fondly up at Bill.

Ah, pensive scholar, what is fame?
A fitful tongue of leaping flame;
A giddy whirlwind's fickle gust,
That lifts a pinch of mortal dust;
A few swift years, and who can show
Which dust was Bill and which was Joe?

The weary idol takes his stand,
Holds out his bruised and aching hand,
While gaping thousands come and go,—
How vain it seems, this empty show!
Till all at once his pulses thrill;—
'Tis poor old Joe's "God bless you, Bill!"

———

And shall we breathe in happier spheres
The names that pleased our mortal ears;
In some sweet lull of harps and song
For earth-born spirits none too long,
Just whispering of the world below
Where this was Bill, and that was Joe?

No matter; while our home is here
No sounding name is half so dear;
When fades at length our lingering day,
Who cares what pompous tombstones say?
Read on the hearts that love us still,
Hic jacet Joe. Hic jacet Bill.[1]

[1]Here lies Joe. Here lies Bill.

OLIVER WENDELL HOLMES
[1809–1894]

LOVE THYSELF LAST

*L*ove thyself last. Look near, behold thy duty
To those who walk beside thee down life's road;
Make glad their days by little acts of beauty,
And them bear the burden of earth's load.

Love thyself last. Look far and find the stranger,
Who staggers 'neath his sin and his despair;
Go lend a hand, and lead him out of danger,
To hights where he may see the world is fair.

Love thyself last. The vastnesses above thee
Are filled with Spirit Forces, strong and pure.
And fervently, these faithful friends shall love thee:
Keep thou thy watch o'er others, and endure.

Love thyself last; and oh, such joy shall thrill thee,
As never yet to selfish souls was given.
Whate'er thy lot, a perfect peace will fill thee,
And earth shall seem the ante-room of Heaven.

Love thyself last, and thou shall grow in spirit
To see, to hear, to know, and understand.
The message of the stars, lo, thou shall hear it,
And all God's joys shall be at thy command.

ELLA WHEELER WILCOX
[1855–1919]

'TIS THE LAST ROSE OF SUMMER

'Tis the last rose of summer
  Left blooming alone;
All her lovely companions
  Are faded and gone;
No flower of her kindred,
  No rosebud, is nigh,
To reflect back her blushes,
  To give sigh for sigh.

I'll not leave thee, thou lone one,
  To pine on the stem;
Since the lovely are sleeping,
  Go sleep thou with them.
Thus kindly I scatter
  Thy leaves o'er the bed,
Where thy mates of the garden
  Lie scentless and dead.

So soon may I follow
  When friendships decay,
And from Love's shining circle
  The gems drop away!
When true hearts lie wither'd,
  And fond ones are flown,
Oh! who would inhabit
  This bleak world alone?

THOMAS MOORE
[1779–1852]

THE MEETING

After so long an absence
At last we meet again;
Does the meeting give us pleasure
Or does it give us pain?

The tree of life has been shaken,
And but few of us linger now,
Like the prophet's two or three berries
In the top of the uppermost bough.

We cordially greet each other
In the old familiar tone;
And we think, though we do not say it,
How old and gray he is grown!

We speak of a Merry Christmas,
And many a happy New Year;
But each in his heart is thinking
Of those that are not here.

We speak of friends and their fortunes,
And of what they did and said,
Till the dead alone seem living,
And the living alone seem dead.

And at last we hardly distinguish
Between the ghosts and the guests;
And a mist and shadow of sadness
Steals over our merriest jests.

HENRY WADSWORTH LONGFELLOW
[1807–1882]

THE OLD FAMILIAR FACES

I have had playmates, I have had companions,
In my days of childhood, in my joyful school-days;
All, all are gone, the old familiar faces.

I have been laughing, I have been carousing,
Drinking late, sitting late, with my bosom cronies;
All, all are gone, the old familiar faces.

I loved a Love once, fairest among women:
Closed are her doors on me, I must not see her—
All, all are gone, the old familiar faces.

I have a friend, a kinder friend has no man:
Like an ingrate, I left my friend abruptly;
Left him, to muse on the old familiar faces.

Ghost-like I paced round the haunts of my childhood,
Earth seem'd a desert I was bound to traverse,
Seeking to find the old familiar faces.

Friend of my bosom, thou more than a brother,
Why wert not thou born in my father's dwelling?
So might we talk of the old familiar faces.

How some they have died, and some they have
    left me,
And some are taken from me; all are departed;
All, all are gone, the old familiar faces.

CHARLES LAMB
[1775–1834]

❀

*A*nd Ruth said:
"Intreat me not to leave thee,
  Or to return from following after thee:
For whither thou goest, I will go,
  And where thou lodgest, I will lodge.
Thy people shall be my people,
  And thy God my God.
Where thou diest, will I die,
  And there will I be buried.
The Lord do so to me, and more also,
  If ought but death part thee and me."

THE BIBLE

PARTING

If thou dost bid thy friend farewell,
But for one night though that farewell may be,
Press thou his hand in thine.
How canst thou tell how far from thee
Fate or caprice may lead his steps ere that to-morrow
comes?
Men have been known to lightly turn the corner of a
street,
And days have grown to months, and months to
lagging years,
Ere they have looked in loving eyes again.
Parting, at best, is underlaid
With tears and pain.
Therefore, lest sudden death should come between,
Or time, or distance, clasp with pressure firm
The hand of him who goeth forth;
Unseen, Fate goeth too.
Yes, find thou always time to say some earnest word
Between the idle talk,
Lest with thee henceforth,
Night and day, regret should walk.

COVENTRY PATMORE
[1823–1896]

LOVE AND FRIENDSHIP

_L_ove is like the wild rose-brier;
  Friendship like the holly-tree.
The holly is dark when the rose-brier blooms,
  But which will bloom most constantly?

The wild rose-brier is sweet in spring,
  Its summer blossoms scent the air;
Yet wait till winter comes again,
  And who will call the wild-brier fair?

Then, scorn the silly rose-wreath now,
  And deck thee with the holly's sheen,
That, when December blights thy brow,
  He still may leave thy garland green.

EMILY BRONTË
[1818–1848]

TO A DISTANT FRIEND

Why art thou silent! Is thy love a plant
Of such weak fibre that the treacherous air
Of absence withers what was once so fair?
Is there no debt to pay, no boon to grant?
Yet have my thoughts for thee been vigilant—
Bound to thy service with unceasing care,
The mind's least generous wish a mendicant
For nought but what thy happiness could spare.
Speak—though this soft warm heart, once free to hold
A thousand tender pleasures, thine and mine,
Be left more desolate, more dreary cold
Than a forsaken bird's-nest filled with snow
'Mid its own bush of leafless eglantine—
Speak, that my torturing doubts their end may know!

WILLIAM WORDSWORTH
[1770–1850]

I READ, DEAR FRIEND

I read, dear friend, in your dear face
Your life's tale told with perfect grace;
The river of your life, I trace
Up the sun-checkered, devious bed
To the far-distant fountain-head.
Not one quick beat of your warm heart,
Nor thought that came to you apart,
Pleasure nor pity, love nor pain
Nor sorrow, has gone by in vain;
But as some lone, wood-wandering child
Brings home with him at evening mild
The thorns and flowers of all the wild,
From your whole life, O fair and true
Your flowers and thorns you bring with you!

ROBERT LOUIS STEVENSON
[1850–1894]

A TEMPLE TO FRIENDSHIP

"A temple to Friendship," cried Laura, enchanted,
"I'll build in this garden; the thought is divine."
So the temple was built, and she now only wanted
An image of Friendship, to place on the shrine.
So she flew to the sculptor, who sat down before her
An image, the fairest his art could invent;
But so cold, and so dull, that the youthful adorer
Saw plainly this was not the Friendship she meant.
"O, never," said she, "could I think of enshrining
An image whose looks are so joyless and dim;
But yon little god upon roses reclining,
We'll make, if you please, sir, a Friendship of him."
So the bargain was struck; with the little god laden,
She joyfully flew to her home in the grove.
"Farewell," said the sculptor, "you're not the first
                maiden
Who came but for Friendship, and took away Love!"

THOMAS MOORE
[1779–1852]

105

NEW FRIENDS AND OLD FRIENDS

Make new friends, but keep the old;
Those are silver, these are gold.
New-made friendships, like new wine,
Age will mellow and refine.
Friendships that have stood the test—
Time and change—are surely best;
Brow may wrinkle, hair grow gray;
Friendship never knows decay.
For 'mid old friends, tried and true,
Once more we our youth renew.
But old friends, alas! may die;
New friends must their place supply.
Cherish friendship in your breast—
New is good, but old is best;
Make new friends, but keep the old;
Those are silver, these are gold.

ANONYMOUS

TO A YOUTHFUL FRIEND

Few years have pass'd since thou and I
Were firmest friends, at least in name,
And childhood's gay sincerity
Preserved our feelings long the same.

But now, like me, too well thou know'st
What trifles oft the heart recall;
And those who once have loved the most
Too soon forget they loved at all.

And such the change the heart displays,
So frail is early friendship's reign,
A month's brief lapse, perhaps a day's,
Will view thy mind estranged again.

If so, it never shall be mine
To mourn the loss of such a heart;
The fault was Nature's fault, not thine,
Which made thee fickle as thou art.

As rolls the ocean's changing tide,
So human feelings ebb and flow;
And who would in a breast confide,
Where stormy passions ever glow?

It boots not that, together bred,
Our childish days were days of joy:
My spring of life has quickly fled;
Thou, too, hast ceased to be a boy.

And when we bid adieu to youth,
Slaves to the specious world's control,
We sign a long farewell to truth;
That world corrupts the noblest soul.

Ah, joyous season! when the mind
Dares all things boldly but to lie;
When thought ere spoke is unconfined,
And sparkles in the placid eye.

Not so in Man's maturer years,
When Man himself is but a tool;
When interest sways our hopes and fears,
And all must love and hate by rule.

With fools in kindred vice the same,
We learn at length our faults to blend;
And those, and those alone, may claim
The prostituted name of friend.

———

Such is the common lot of man:
Can we then 'scape from folly free?
Can we reverse the general plan,
Nor be what all in turn must be?

No; for myself, so dark my fate
Through every turn of life hath been,
Man and the world so much I hate,
I care not when I quit the scene.

But thou, with spirit frail and light,
Wilt shine awhile, and pass away;
As glow-worms sparkle through the night,
But dare not stand the test of day.

Alas! whenever folly calls
Where parasites and princes meet
(For cherish'd first in royal halls,
The welcome vices kindly greet),

Ev'n now thou'rt nightly seen to add
One insect to the fluttering crowd;
And still thy trifling heart is glad
To join the vain, and court the proud.

There dost thou glide from fair to fair,
Still simpering on with eager haste,
As flies along the gay parterre,
That taint the flowers they scarcely taste.

But say, what nymph will prize the flame
Which seems, as marshy vapours move,
To flit along from dame to dame,
An ignis-fatuus gleam of love?

What friend for thee, howe'er inclined,
Will deign to own a kindred care?
Who will debase his manly mind,
For friendship every fool may share?

In time forbear; amidst the throng
No more so base a thing be seen;
No more so idly pass along;
Be something, any thing, but—mean.

GEORGE GORDON, LORD BYRON
[1788–1824]

———

THE HUMAN TOUCH

'Tis the human touch in this world that counts,
   The touch of your hand and mine,
Which means far more to the fainting heart
   Than shelter and bread and wine;
For shelter is gone when the night is o'er,
   And bread lasts only a day,
But the touch of the hand and the sound of the voice
   Sing on in the soul alway.

SPENCER MICHAEL FREE

A WAYFARING SONG

O who will walk a mile with me
   Along life's merry way?
A comrade blithe and full of glee,
Who dares to laugh out loud and free
And let his frolic fancy play,
Like a happy child, through the flowers gay
That fill the field and fringe the way
   Where he walks a mile with me.

And who will walk a mile with me
   Along life's weary way?
A friend whose heart has eyes to see
The stars shine out o'er the darkening lea,
And the quiet rest at the end o' the day—
A friend who knows, and dares to say,
The brave, sweet words that cheer the way
   Where he walks a mile with me.

With such a comrade, such a friend,
I fain would walk till journey's end,
Through summer sunshine, winter rain,
And then?—Farewell, we shall meet again!

HENRY VAN DYKE
[1853–1933]

FRIENDSHIP NEEDS NO STUDIED
PHRASES

Friendship needs no studied phrases,
  Polished face, or winning wiles;
Friendship deals no lavish praises,
  Friendship dons no surface smiles.

Friendship follows Nature's diction,
  Shuns the blandishments of art,
Boldly severs truth from fiction,
  Speaks the language of the heart.

Friendship favors no condition,
  Scorns a narrow-minded creed,
Lovingly fulfills its mission,
  Be it word or be it deed.

Friendship cheers the faint and weary,
  Makes the timid spirit brave,
Warms the erring, lights the dreary,
  Smooths the passage to the grave.

Friendship—pure, unselfish friendship,
  All through life's allotted span,
Nurtures, strengthens, widens, lengthens,
  Man's relationship with man.

ANONYMOUS

FRIENDSHIP

Friendship. peculiar boon of heav'n,
The noble mind's delight and pride,
To men and angels only giv'n,
To all the lower world denied.

Thy gentle flows of guiltless joys
On fools and villains ne'er descend;
In vain for thee the tyrant sighs,
And hugs a flatterer for a friend.

Directress of the brave and just,
O guide us through life's darksome way!
And let the tortures of mistrust
On selfish bosoms only prey.

Nor shall thine ardors cease to glow,
When souls to peaceful climes remove:
What rais'd our virtue here below,
Shall aid our happiness above.

SAMUEL JOHNSON
[1709–1784]

INDEX

OF AUTHORS

INDEX

OF FIRST LINES

ABOUT THE AUTHOR

With a degree in English literature, KATHLEEN BLEASE first served as an editor for two major publishing houses before starting out on her own as a freelance book editor and writer. Over the span of her career, she has written on a variety of topics—such as health, education, home improvements, and parenthood—and edited books that have won acclaim throughout the country.

Five years ago, her love unexpectedly knocked on her front door and introduced himself, and Kathleen's vision of life changed forever. Today she is a full-time mother of two small children, often writing and researching with a little one in her arms. Her marriage and young family provide her with a never-ending resource of examples of the power of faith, family, and friends—material she instills in her essays, articles, and collections.

Kathleen's previous collection, *Love in Verse: Classic Poems of the Heart,* is a *Boston Book Review* bestseller. Her other collection is *A Mother's Love: Classic Poems Celebrating the Maternal Heart.*

She lives with her husband, Roger, and their two children in the historic district of Easton, Pennsylvania.

Give the gift of poetry and prayer to someone you love!

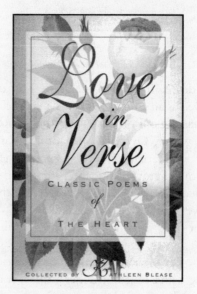

An incomparable collection of beauty and grace, *Love in Verse* pays fitting tribute to the world's most treasured emotion.

Strephon kissed me in the spring,

Robin in the fall,

But Colin only looked at me

And never kissed at all.

Strephon's kiss was lost in jest,

Robin's lost in play,

But the kiss in Colin's eyes

Haunts me night and day.

—Sara Teasdale

COLLECTED BY *Kathleen Blease*

A Mother's Love

CLASSIC POEMS CELEBRATING
THE MATERNAL HEART

Always giving, mothers seldom ask for
anything in return.
Now here's a moving celebration of love
that will touch and warm any mother's
heart. . . .

. . . coming in May 1999!

Over my heart, in the days that are flown,

No love like my mother-love ever has

shown,

No other worship abides and endures—

Faithful, unselfish, and patient like yours.

—Elizabeth Akers Allen

And don't miss this very special volume
by Ailene Eberhard:

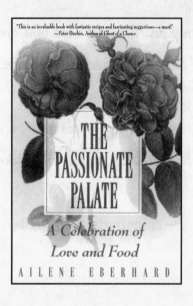

Nothing fans the fires of love like good
food that is lovingly prepared and served
with affection. This tempting mating of
food and love makes culinary wooing a
snap, providing a feast of twenty-eight ele-
gant dinner menus organized by season
that is sure to nourish the body and stir
the senses. . . .